Free Radicals: American Poets Before Their First Books

Free Radicals: American Poets Before Their First Books

edited by
Jordan Davis and Sarah Manguso

Subpress
Honolulu/Oakland/New York

Published in the United States by
  Subpress

Cover design by Tanya Bezreh, 2004;
Additional cover design work by Chi Ho.

Library of Congress Cataloging-in-Publication Data

Free radicals : American poets before their first books / edited by
Jordan Davis and Sarah Manguso.
    p. cm.
  Includes index.
  ISBN 1-930068-23-9 (alk. paper)
  1. American poetry--21st century. I. Davis, Jordan. II. Manguso,
Sarah, 1974-
PS617.F74 2004
811'.608--dc22

                                    2004006284

TABLE OF CONTENTS

I once asked the poetry buyer for Barnes & Noble what book he was looking for that didn't exist yet. He responded almost immediately that there was a crying need for an annual anthology of work by newly minted MFAs.

This isn't that book. Some of the writers included here do have graduate degrees in writing, but some do not.

Poetry, it must be remembered, is the least important of the arts. It makes nothing happen, and I don't mean "nothing that is not there/and the nothing that is."

Poetry is fundamentally an attack on everything we hold dear. An attack it is so easy to avoid there is no defense budget that even begins to consider it. Just don't read it! Millions take this precaution every day.

But what about the benighted tens. Aye. It is they these poets are hoping to catch at a vulnerable moment. As my co-editor has mentioned, free radicals tend to promote unpredictable reactions. The health conscious take vitamin tablets to defeat them.

The government of poetryland — the judges of prizes, editors of magazines, tenured pedalows, gatekeepers and kingmakers — has a much surer way to neutralize these dangerous presences. It brings them into the fold. It folds them into the batter. It batters them into unsolicited submission.

It has happened to the editors. We believe it will happen to the contributors soon as well (Jennifer Knox's collection was accepted by Soft Skull Press shortly after her inclusion here; it is scheduled for publication sometime in the zero-decade).

Boris Pasternak wrote that to know what a poet means, it is important to have read his or her work from the beginning — to have seen the stumbles and the first felicitous phrases. Again, this isn't that book. These are accomplished, strange and turbulent poems by writers we are happy to have caught up with somewhere in the middle of their development, but before their emergence is universally acknowledged. Heads up.

— *Jordan Davis*

Once you've made your mark on history those who can't will be so grateful they'll turn it into a cage for you.
—Lester Bangs, *"Thinking the Unthinkable About John Lennon"* (1980)

What excites me about these poets is that, beside their talent, they are all blessed with the terrible freedom of not yet having published books.

Even the best- and best-received first books provoke a set of expectations of what the poet should produce, or is capable of producing, next. Sudden fame tends to demolish the lives of adolescent film stars, and poets, even with their tiny fame, do not escape the effects of the infinitely reflecting mirror of a readership. A Hegelian synthesis between poets' first books and their first criticisms occurs not once, not twice, but forever.

In the field of physics, free radicals are unstable molecules containing odd numbers of electrons and tending toward violent and unpredictable chemical reactions. In the field of poetry, instability can often yield truer work than facility can. A mature poet's facility with his craft can threaten the genuineness of his product — one that turns into a celebration of skill rather than a necessary foray into a mysterious world. This is not to say that all emerging poets are afire and that all mature poets are shallow — but only that public validation and expectation increase as a poet's career continues, and that the threat of writing to an audience becomes only more present a danger as time passes and renown increases.

I take special joy in reading work by these poets who, while already setting their new stars into the poetical firmament, are not mired in the stability-enforcing, niche-assigning public consciousness. The 18 poets represented in this volume are only a fraction of the free radicals making poetry in America in 2004. I hope you enjoy their good work.

—*Sarah Manguso*

B.J. ATWOOD-FUKUDA

The Wreck of the *Platonic*

The guy at the next table reminded her of her first serious boyfriend, but even as the word *serious* surfaced to the chattery part of her brain that was already watching someone hear her tell the story long since gone barnacle-encrusted as myth, already hearing her own voice run it out like Morse code on the quiet of a moonless, star-splattered sky, she realized as if pronouncing it for the very first time what a euphemism *serious* was, I mean it might have served some purpose in the early sixties when anyone would have understood that it meant the first boy she'd *fucked*, not loved, since in those days girls rarely fucked their first loves, assuming that girls back then loved for the first time at thirteen or fourteen the way they do now only more intensely, if anything, since girls back then not only didn't assume that the relationship, which they didn't call it, if any, would be consummated but, if they'd been raised in those days of the double standard to be, well, *nice*, they were mostly scared silly of the very idea notwithstanding the depth of their craving, the intensity of their fascination with the throbbing flesh for which it, mere "very idea" in the starch voices of a million middle-class white moms, was but a limp stand-in, a shriveled shill, a most unreasonable, wimpy facsimile thereof. So they built the ship *Platonic* to warn us not to screw; what it had to do with Plato, we didn't have a clue. Poor Plato, alas, lamented the incapacity of chairs to approach the ideal of chairness; no chair, however hard it might try, could ever achieve in his eyes the beauty of that naked, unmediated state. Poor Plato, obsessed with chairs. No wonder she and her girlfriends had wondered why abstinence was called *Platonic* or, more precisely, why it meant not-fucking, since if they'd run into the word at all it would have been somebody's uncle in AA, and who ever talked about that back then; and finally, when they got to philosophy in school, how the hell Platonic got conjured from Plato, a man who had once lived and breathed and jerked himself off, they supposed, against the backs of chairs in various states of imperfection — rocky, rickety, rocking — the doctor in the deep blue sea only knew. Poor Plato, lured off his true and proper course, fetched up on a floating slagheap of sophistry, hoisted on a pinnacle of pieties arch and brittle as ice. O they built the ship Platonic to warn us not to screw, and they thought we'd get on board and enjoy the frigid view. Were they wrong. Young girls and boys saw right through their parents' ploys, husbands and wives had to reassess their lives. Was it sad? no doubt, o so sad, she thought as she eyed the guy at the next table over and watched that clone of her first serious boyfriend lean back in his chair so it squealed and moaned under his weight, so its legs thrust up to reveal at once the fragility and force of the attachment, the dazzling impermanence of the greater whole — a form which surpassed, in its corporeal perfection, any ideal to which it might have sought or been forbidden to aspire. O spire, o pinnacle of pieties erupting on the sweet breath of night, plunging into the dark, fragrant, teeming, blooming sea. How they lied, yee-hah! how we laughed and cried, how they sighed when that great ship went down.

Ballybunion

You hike along the tops of cliffs above the sea, over miles of green meadows dotted with buttercups and ramshackle fences. The lumpy ground squishes beneath your feet. In other places it feels hard, strewn as it is with rubble and rock. The landscape offers no hint of the startling danger you find hidden there: holes, in the grass, in the earth, some of them barely the circumference of a bucket, others as big as a backyard swimming pool; not crevasses but black holes, unfenced, unmarked, plunging hundreds of feet through the earth to the sea. You learn, after the first few you've stumbled upon and almost fallen into, how to spot one from some distance away: You study the attitude of the grass, check the tufts for the subtle darkness rising at their roots which would betray the presence of a crater below, even as the shadow in an x-ray portends a tumor; and as you draw closer, you hear the sea pounding against its prison of walls, distant, muffled, small as the voice of a trapped bird. You spot the bloated body of a sheep at the bottom of one of these wells. You ask a man you meet wandering the moor with his own sheep if animals, or children, don't fall into them with some frequency; you muse on how strange it seems that the holes are not marked in any way. He tells you the locals know the area so well it rarely happens, that their children learn from them. As for animals, he says, they have a sixth sense, you know. The students, young lads, are another kettle of fish — they get tipsy and come up here and carry on and before you know it, someone's gone missing.

Behold the minefield of your waking dreams. A dirtpath winds through meadows and woods, more or less in a single direction. You move along it alone. You scan every rock and weed and flower, in vain, for the slightest hint of what you know to lurk beneath the blandish, commonplace earth. You pick your way in a haze of white fear fueled by the futility of your very approach, yet never do you dare to run or dance, lest a mine explode in your face. When it does, the dream shatters: a cataclysm unmatched in your imagination. This is the ur-disaster, the one to which all later calamities seek comparison. The one in whose sere light all others pale. The one that sets you free.

JIM BEHRLE

White Album

white circle, white line white X, warm white
like parchment of like a scroll.
flick white, carve it up into pieces
like nothing, white canvas-flavored.
rushing water, white like speeding.
rapids blur all white,
like forest, fuck and flame.
million stars aswirl. paper a grid of shadow
in daylight — everything.
glint across a knee then higher.
white toward midnight and summer.
you feel and flash, you stumble and fall.
moonlight, day, dusk, sun-up, drip.
five lines of white against a mirror.
white, more white, a camera sucks it in, an eye.
neon, sweet, permanent.

black and white as that night,
slow motion and right.
as a baseball sailing toward the wall —
a homerun or a double?
a homerun, hallelujah for us.
white as Boston — wrong as that is.
oh, I want to sparkle and be forgiven like
a clean white undershirt like toothpaste,
a smile. white as absence, as dirty,
cold, a wing unfurling, dirty as
the exploding sun.

white as pussy in starlight, in raindrops.
than blank and blank, blanker than the
blankest blank, blanking against — shadow
disguised as, homonym for,
comma comma space.
white between and in an "m" or a "p."
the white I make now, white on your chin
wiped away quickly. how white
I am, how late it is,

fucking hooray for white
circle, star and fountain, dusk and suck.

smoke for white, headlight guilt and
sorrow. hello, white, sweet thing. substitute
for blue and yellow, hello white, calm white,
clinging white,

as long and as wrong as you are,
years of nothing but you,
tears clear of you, a sound as solid,
a horizon blinds, fuck you white,
hold me white, stop all in white,
white down, white falls, white quits, breaks
white, just a white, white cut of you.

Beacon Arms

from this moment on, what is
    To be Left Behind?
        bread crumbs, Post-its

Should I get married and be Good or puke?

      Trample and buzz forward Solo.

Upon reading this Maybe you'll feel less chased
    I gotta go. You gotta go?
    We better go.

Very brass, the stonework of the Morning After,

Is it wrong to blow the Students and Tourists?
    And who's asking the
    tough questions These days

Most don't remember birthdays. From now on
    we'll keep the gears
    clean.

There's a call on 1 or 2.

It's a future you, fucking with you now.

Going to the chapel, hunting cheap wine and eucharist

Becuz No One's looking and you can:
    induct magic into the Hall

Good Night, All You Ships at Sea, You

We're on Sorrow Watch engulfed by Scorpion Bowls

haunted repeatedly in Dreams by Dave Letterman

when it's my funeral I'll want La Cucaracha
                    and F-16 flyovers

First choose your weight in water: essence
                        of mango or Youth

No one dies with you, regardless of riches
                    or recent poll numbers

Ex-girlfriends gather to march huffily Toward shore

Adapting to the new Ban on hullabaloo

At the first signs   Yet agape, Shudder to think of

Inflamed tonsils, they Strike
                    You down walking your Delightful coast

Dateline Egypt: Could have had more Pyramids
if only we'd Worked together

            Pass a bottle of Nile,

while watching soldiers fortify
            every Ferris Wheel or Tilt-a-Whirl

O to be the one   To chase off the Frankensteins
                    we built

Hooray for our impossible Demands,

shrugged off   Undershirt

            and clean Sheets misplaced

The Charm of the Highway Strip

objects in the mirror are mirrors
   backbeats help strip it clean
      we're watching Al-Jazeera & getting high
   beneath a gray anvil of history
where are the poets? check the discos

ask a stranger I'm fast and danger
   madly past shiny convenience and
      cute but reductive theories of inaction
   come take a seat upon my anger sword
sonic booms that got stopped by God

they had big dicks for hearts
   black telephones to light the way
      in thievespeak, sorry, how would you say
   "go ahead, gas up the family tank"
our boys march over hymens to victory

34.57: from *Twenty-Six Friends, That's the Same as Your Age*

14.

Am I a French poet who writes poems twenty years too early?

Am I a Chilean who instructs rocks and has only praise for bee stings?

Or am I an American who makes himself in delusions?

Who patents insults of the perfect technique?

18.

Does he call one dog Rimbaud and the other Hölderlin?

Does his beard-on-fire escape the perimeter of our foresight?

And does he read the jogger's manual as he converts from religion to religion?

19.

How far does Death see?

To the city from the country?

To Paris from Baltimore?

And does it alter his voice's fatefulness?

And does it make my dreams deshroud themselves?

20.

Where there's beer is there also the alarum within of my personality?

Do you say, "Where's that shite-ing poet?" as I walk my internal concourses?

Or do you write my epithet on all the walls to embarrass me out of existence?

21.

Am I a linguist of self-translation?

Do I placate my inner selves just to find meaning?

Does an orange eat you, or you it?

And how would you know unless a child tugged your sleeve?

22.

Every poem is lonely and en route, you say?

Did you say that, poet Paul Celan?

Or was it the hush in my heart finally standing up for itself?

25.

Is this the story of the left and right hands?

In love, but always in opposing quadrants?

And hiding their secret desires while we sleep in wandering beds?

26.

When you turned 26, did it feel like anything?

Or did the day pass quietly?

Like a fly in the other room you'll never even see?

Like those who walk with you, but always one street down
and one street over?

42.24

That girl's breasts distracted everyone at the baseball game. The umpire frequently mistook the count. The pitcher had no cares as to the location or delivery of his pitches. Nor did the batters appear to mind striking out at all. As a sidenote, a TV colorman did make one insightful commentary, as follows: "Though I owe much of my life's happiness to the splendor of this beautiful and honored game, there are times when we submit to a force beyond our control, no matter how it might compromise our relationship to those things we hold dear. I confess that, at this point, I am entirely invested in the magnanimity of this woman's bosom and have no further concerns other than just to stare at her chest for as long as I live. And, if 'as long as I live' is only for the next minute, it'll have been worth it, for this moment could span ages if it were judged in terms of truth and beauty, the meanings of which I have just now understood."

47.57

I remember when they opened the Gaza Strip Club
amidst fanfare and protest in 1988 —
or, Year of the Parent-Teacher Conference
according to this calendar for a religion
whose doctrine holds
that honesty is merely one of the policies
and the most important decisions are game-time decisions.

I was just eight, but already familiar with
the *Let's Go Guide to American Castles*

and a nonfiction epic called *History of Sleep*,
written by a man who described himself as an immigrant
despite having been born and raised
among the many articulate forests
of a Connecticut highway strip.

It was just about that time I had my first communion,
held at the Senior Citizens' Center
in a part of town known for its easy-to-read coinage
and a statue of the earliest known human
to have invested in term life insurance.

The priest called my name amidst the ambient noise
of Bingo and respirators,
mispronouncing it in a way that made it sound impossibly unfamiliar,
like the Welsh for anything
or the native word for a South American fish
that'd die instantly in our markedly colder waters.

It makes me think of how
there are places I'll never go —
be it oil rig or Namibia —
no matter how long I live.

And when I'm asked that question,
"Would you choose to live forever?"
I always answer yes,

because there are infinite stats to calculate each season,
like the Walk to Strikeout ratios of journeymen relievers
and the exact amount of depression I feel
whenever I'm asked to elaborate
on the strength and diversity of my investment portfolio.

It's always possible you could get your own sports radio show
and find out first hand
just how much players and coaches
want to put points up on the board.

"It's a struggle each time,
but we hope to play hard and get the *W*,"
they say at every turn
like the earliest models of robots
programmed for one task only.

But those are the robots I like.
And if there were a movie in which they took over the world,
I'd like that movie,
starring a little-known actor in his first leading role
who realizes that robots are just like us,
maybe not in how they look or talk,
but that they've got needs, too,
like processors that won't freeze up
and like dramatically wider sidewalks
along all these city streets
so there's room to walk two-by-two
with their larger robot bodies.

Will Run Like Rabbits for Food

I lied when I said I'd get back to entertaining myself,
    as you can see; There are no teethmarks in the alleyway
    or lights on deep through the video store. Only thing
  in the room arranged like an opening are my boots — They'd make
the perfect b&w blownup photograph
    at a fiendish thingy, where one lets her hair do the talking.

Whatshername suggested I adopt large lollipops & a new
    posture. I was ballsout about it for eight minutes.
Would you believe I'm shaking?
It's cool — I dreamt I was either dying or concise,
    & not a jot of it was all my fault,
  so I hit the couch: Red rocket, Static cover.

The middle bit, my neck, is booking to church in a galliard,
    reflecting the time I got up, who I started calling…
  Anything tree-tapped would do; I'm talking Hard Science here.
Okay History — I'll take History —
    Someday I'll wish I knew more about Rome:
    Possible't's stuffed up in the days getting longer.

It's an evening that can't even be solved by pointing & laughing
    at books for people who believe in angels. Better to take
  a short bath than pack, & to take a long bath than go anywhere —
It's the new style, that'll see you on the aisle,
    when we're all not ducking ice from our friends in back —
    It's the last bit of tape verse the weight of a saved jeans ad.

Anthelmintic

On the eerily StarWars campus
of Boston College, Samantha was not speaking
   to me. I had pointed out her fake
British accent to the empty tour...

She was tiny. She was clicking away
from me in every direction furiously —
  Up & down the stone stairs... amid the drifts
    of rotting leaves... Hell, amid the bright flyers.

        I was terrified as
there seemed to be lacrosse sticks everywhere, & Chicky
   was finding the live leaves; putting the live leaves
   in her hair, screaming "Let me tell you

about children of divorce," her hair so
full of berries, "We are always apologizing!" The car
  we came in was blue... I could sense the sea-spray...
The girls had made me eat rich food & I

was sick — In the alcoves
these kids seemed to know each other too & some
   had long coats. I was fascinated with the
  sky — I thought "This is what travelling

will do." Samantha sat down...
Chicky twirled her thin green skirts in the white
    light... Elissa said "Let's go now —
Let's go & see B.U."

8 O'Clock Defeat, Approximately

There's a shuffle in the thin fall morning
    breaking to a confused perfume —
  At the very, very outset of a week,
     by the most echoing & clinical of rooms —
  In the moment when a high-modernist penguin
     with an insouciant beak
   does not fly through the door, without warning,
     & She turns, lovely and thin,
away.

Or with a hardcovered & deeply violet book
    containing essays on 'Nonsense in Cook,'
 it does not not sit right next to her;
         & damned if it don't stay.

Second thoughts & second looks then
     branch off in geometric heat:
Forming an undetected and bothersome urchin
to anyfool walking past
in a heat-vision mask
  with a pointing finger & stilts on their feet.

    On a whim, the morning gets hotter —
   There is again that thing in my chest —
Heavily, heavily, the pretty girl's pen
    gives a winking teeter-totter
 on the fatal, rounded edge of her desk,
  much to the leering interest of all:

The Bird himself removes the crosses from the wall
  When the pearlgirl recrosses her blackpants for him.

It's Just As Well About Heather

Sarah's thinner friend,
because all her heroines were groundbreaking female serial killers.
    She hit that one boyfriend with a brick in the
        woods; took his car with all his money in it.
    She tricked that other into drinking bleach;
cried anyway all the way to the hospital.

But still she was the perfect, for Boston in March,
in a little limegreen of a thing, as I remember it:
    The headsets all in a row & down the stairs
waiting on that watery pudding.

Also she was from Mercer Island,
if you can believe it (where Dave Grohl is from), & did
    quite well for a while at the antique shop thanks
        to Sarah (who once saw Jerry Hall there). None

        of her Simmons histrionics with the security guards,
in a heap on the floor of some Something-&-Gender Class,
crying "Let them escort me, then!"

Are you an atheist with a fireplace glee?
Yes, pirouetting over fenced-in walkways.
        & so

sure she wanted us to move to Paris,
where she would become a whore & I develop
        consumption (to the best of my efforts, anyway)...

Would she have tried to kill me?

Probably.

But she wore a lot of thigh-highs, had
    a very sexy German last name, & — who knows? —
may have actually been
    as talented, or as in love with Trotsky, as she claimed.

Sterling Park

Lady was her name and she was sniffing up the horseflies on the hill
as well as the sun and the fountain and the Spanish tiles and

the dragonflies and the other German Shepherds whose ears
pricked up at each squeak of a sneaker on the basketball court above

muffled by the leaves and hidden below underneath the telephone pole
the directions man hollered things through the traffic noise like

turn right man no straight up and to your right and
whoa hold on just a minute okay you can come on now

the fog was bright as day it lit up most of Sausalito
two sailboats stole their way out of the pier and into a certain siesta

Lady's man smoked a cigarette on a green park bench where
out from the earth came the gray legs of an evergreen that

slept down the hill its slovenly tentacles rubbing variegated brush
limbs encumbered by the spirited deciduous and coniferous

by the carnivorous ivy overtaking some of its legs
as Lady's man leaves with his Lady (a countess among dog denizens)

Sausalito's all gone and the seagulls hover like kites
a menagerie of sailboats moseys over the rooftops and into the abyss

the bus poems

somebody's welding
a bus to the
black sky

I'd crumble too
if I
were that sky

somebody's building
a skyscraper
disco

bang bang
bang

a cigarette
a sneeze at 7:10

listen to how
the world shakes

*

hark
how the lone tree
fills up
with
nesters

I love
the bird that's
in love

almost making
the same music
as the bus
turning the corner

*

one star
to be seen
Venus maybe

count how
many lights
on the face
of that building

before one
goes off
or on

where is
my bus

*

nobody
but the bus

nothing
but the music
of the trash bucket
dragged
over gravel

*

a streetlamp
and those
screeching
bird buses

oilspill
continents
on asphalt

cigarette
lagoons

buses
hooked up
to a moonless web
that hovers
over the streets

*

the bus
does not
arrive

I am
angry to
write
in this
pleasant
starlight

*

sure
the 38
is late

but how many
stories
fly
into the
constellations

from this
bus bench

never else
seen
or told

which is okay
I suppose

big words

boredom
the fog rolls over the bay
the bus rolls with it
my nose stuck inside a heavy book

one fiery red maple rises up
from behind a hedgerow
and disappears

turn-on (with most of a line by Spicer)

when your body brushed against me and I
looked into the hole of your ear for something
that was not there but felt its presence anyway a
funnel cloud its lobe a skinned almond I couldn't resist I

took you to bed in the soggy brush I took you to a
stranger's bed we danced until the milkweed broke apart
beside our exhausted funnel cakes it was only a
coincidence that you pushed your way through to the

back of the bus just to brush against my shoulder
where I ignored your darkest eyes with my hard-on
reading word for heartrending word the entire history of
civilization trying not to burn a hole clean through it

All the flutterlings gone.

But nodded off enough.
Only the breeze. Dull.
With white sky.

Walked the beach
into the windmill
& slept for days on dunes

listening drowsing
to the ocean until a
bird juttered me up.

So now I sit in the
nowhere section —
the other side of the

road from the
golf course.
Very quiet.

I'm so lucky.
To have
this peace.

Ceci n'est pas une pipe.

I cannot draw
the blinds

headlights
from what I know
is a garage
and jetplane lights

are pulled
into the
dark sweet
smoke of night

the blinds
are drawn

Theofilos
painted golden
loaves of bread
that stand up
on end

but the loaves
do not
fall
because

"only real loaves
fall down...

painted ones
stay where you
put them"

it is a painting

the blinds
are not
drawn

but a
Tweetie Bird balloon
bobs up
and down
behind the hedge

and the moon
does not suffer

a spot
of ink

trilogy

Intro

monday night i went to the san francisco art institute to see nathaniel dorsky's silent film trilogy, which consists of *triste, variations,* and *arbor vitae.* packed house. clark coolidge sat right in front of me. bill berkson, who'd told me this was a must-not-miss event, did the welcome introductions. nathaniel dorsky explained that, though folks like to call this set of films a "trilogy," they are really just variations on a theme with the inherent differences brought on by the fact that he was a different person when he made each film (the first one was basically shot in the '70s/'80s, the second in the later '80s, the third in the '90s). the first 2 films were beautiful. about 5 minutes into the 3rd and newest film, the projector bulb "burned a hole" into the film — an abrupt stop. a 2nd attempt was made — film mended, rethreaded & started from beginning. only a few frames after the spot where the film broke the first time, it burned/broke again. i didn't wait to see if a 3rd attempt was made. the first two films were beautiful. the day before which was sunday it was seventy degrees. i went for a walk through golden gate park. and sat down in shakespeare garden until dusk.

Shakespeare Garden

the sun's going
huge mosquito
poking thru my shirt

i'm thinking about heritage
in shakespeare garden
and the word "sump"

a couple walks by
talking "waves" and "rays"
and "perpendiculars"

the flowers under the
japanese trees: butters, bloods,
purples, pinks, whites

dandelions
(this is february!)
flowers blooming, trees barren

i wonder how
happy i am
(ready for spring)

smoke sky/no clouds
bark (trees and dogs)
fountain — nope it's a sundial

several firs & other greens
that never go away
(grandpa died quickly

after woodsplitting
one winter day)
i'm not at all tired

after Triste

overlooking lit ants
or streetlamps
from way up here

next to a coffeeshop
(look there's the artist i
asked to dance & his coffee)

i'm humbled by the moving
pictures fluttered with:
wrens, wending rivulets,

pleasure suns, acid trips,
legs walking, white
birds flying seen through

mesh of trees, more water,
raindrops on windshields
(the different colors),

prowling siamese cat
(reminds me of a painting
i just saw of an empty

swimming pool
symbolizing death),
bricks (matter of fact),

entwined water hoses
(without water),
anything beautiful to

look at that you wouldn't
ordinarily think of as
beautiful (or maybe you would),

faces, places,
it doesn't matter
that the bulb

sizzled the film
click-click
erroneously threaded

i make my escape
before the trilogy
ends

not like these folks for smokes
or pleasures of restrooms or coffee
but air night

look at the city ants
breathe & wonder if
the movie

has split
into   two   new
beautiful   movies

let's try something

when the sky blinks
like a satin-covered

canvas in the middle
of a midnight meadow

with the obsidian wind
blowing like rocks

when the washing
machine works but

the dryer doesn't and
Maria asks "How do

YOU write?" and you say
"I'm using less space"

Rothko

The sun came
up today. It
burned an

ebon ocean
into the mud.

Office Depot parking lot

at the crosswalk
a fuzzy apparition

the moon
over the
bottlebrush
blooms

(the green hand
glows so
okay to cross

into wet black
parking lot)

into three layers
of clouds:

1) fat circus peanuts
    floating on top

2) the beautifullest layer
    is the orange city
    that duplicates the
    hoary one below   ·

3) the fog beyond
    Embarcadero
    on top of
    the water

before the day's
blood leaves
the sky

an orange flicker
on the sluiced asphalt

a paperclip

drowned
from fall's
first rain

The Vote

Eating spinach makes my teeth squeak.
Perhaps moreso when I am reading certain newsflashes.
I have almost gotten used to artificial sweetener.
And still manage to fail at birthday surprises.

I left a stick of gum under David's bed.
He said thank you it was "tasty" — so tongue-in-cheek!
At 1:25 pm I wonder who else is driving under the influence.
And how November can be so tepid.

District 2 is shaped like Florida upside-down.
I just read a poem that ends with an upside-down cake.
A show of hands: Who can remember the Berlin Wall?
My mother demos meat products at Sam's Wholesale.

We're all inoculated for the I LOVE YOU virus.
47% of potential voters couldn't agree more.
I think I'll wash this down with a lemon.
And pack my tattered luggage for a slow boat to nowhere.

Cinema Yosemite

1.

(I want a love)

precise
as Kubrick

(like in) the movie
we watched
that night

Kar-wai Wong's
In the Mood for Love

what pleasures
in textures & all possible
patterns

I hold your hand
for longer than usual

while the
lovesick couple
on the silver screen
refuses to do so

two impeccably dressed
unconsummated
mammals

Tony Leung's
eyes

Maggie Cheung's
silhouette
upon a curtain

she's certain
she

will fall apart

2.

the next day
while hiking
to Lower
Yosemite Falls

snapshot
a six-point buck
munching

its nose
snow-nuzzled

and then
a doe
several of them
(does)
dawdle
for our photo lens

and earlier
Ansel Adams's
orange
El Capitan
lighted
by the sunrise
hidden
behind Bridalveil Falls

or thereabouts

and the next day's hike
through
almost virgin snow

to the bridge
under
Vernal Falls

I'm not with you

I am with you

take a picture
of the water
falling

hand me
your hand

3.

in the
hotel room

because there
is
a hotel room

with two beds

we watch
the remake
of *Doctor Dolittle*

4.

at home
after Yosemite
we watch
together

Curt McDowell's
Thundercrack!

it's an
uproarious
art-porn flick
from the '70s

a two-&-a-half-hour
magnum opus

with
Marion Eaton
and
Mookie Blodgett

filmed so
perfectly
primitive

it's hard to tell
what is
being said

somewhere
the bears
move slowly
over
snowtrails

the mountain lions
slink carnally
into caverns

5.

snowcaps

all sorts of
beautiful people
in hot tubs

panorama
of sky
some color
you'd never imagined

bedeviled
by sensuous
fog-roll

rolling

over duvets

mountains
so populous
and full of doggerel

skin so

I haven't slipped
and fallen

the treacherous
snowtrail

fallen
finding heat I'm

please (lower
the camera)

in the mood
I'm in the mood

for love

Il Massimo del Panino

Have you ever
read a poem
that made you cry

sitting in an
Italian restaurant
eating a

spinaci e fontina
panino
across from a

man with a
mustache drinking
a Diet Coke

while another man
walks in, arms-
outstretched shouting

to the owner
"Donald Trump!
Donald Trump!"

and next to you
two tablesful
of students

one loudly
letting loose with
"I no playboy!"

as the
others spatter
sweet lexical

nothings in
German, Italian,
and Japanese?

The Painted Ladies

The risotto at Caffé Proust
is pretty good.

Redheads usually sunburn
easily.

The sky's blue,
but lightly buttered.

And the pastel faces
line up behind the drycleaners.

These are not the Painted Ladies
from down the street.

But they are really very
Victorian.

can't oh

please bring
back the

insignificant
lakes

from the poem
I started

just yes-
terday

I called them all
but gone

how wrong I
should have been

Seeds

About noon on Avenue C yesterday, I was stopped by a boy who looked about 7 or 8.

Boy: Excuse me, do you know where I could get me some seeds?

Me: Seeds?

Boy: Yeah, you know, seeds.

Me: Uh, well, there's a hardware store right over there, but it looks closed … Go to Ace Hardware on 1st Avenue near 4th, I guess.

Boy: Which way is 1st Avenue?

Me (*pointing to the right*): That way.

Boy (*looking confused*): What avenue is this?

Me: Avenue C. If I were you I'd just turn right here. You have to pass B, A, and then 1st. Cross 1st, then turn left and you'll see the store. Ace Hardware, OK?

Boy's Probable Mom (*a huge black woman, until now unnoticed, hanging out across the street and one block down, shouting*): WHAT YOU DOIN!

Boy (*turning the corner at 4th Street*): GETTING SEEDS!

5-Year-Old Girls Encountered

1. In the Very Back of the Bus

Girl: Mommy do you remember yesterday when Daddy was talking about someone died?

(*adult voice says something that can't be heard*)

Girl: But do you remember when Daddy said someone died?

(*adult voice says something that can't be heard*)

Girl: No. Remember when somebody died?

(*adult voice says something that can't be heard*)

Girl: A man! Yes someone died. He DID die!

(*adult voice says something that can't be heard*)

Girl: Every day. Every day! A man!

(*adult voice says something that can't be heard*)

Girl: Mommy, Mommy, I know everything!

(*adult voice says something that can't be heard*)

Girl: Mommy look at me I know everything!

2. In the Penn Station Bathroom

Girl: These are magic! They are magic Mommy! I don't want to go in with you!

Mommy: Well, now how about we wait for the big one and then you can stand far away from it while I go, okay?

Girl: But Mommy, they're magic! I don't like the magic ones!

(*a sensor-activated toilet flushes*)

Mommy: See, now that wasn't so loud! These aren't so loud, honey.

Girl: But are they all going to sound like that?

TONYA FOSTER

A Folktale

A father stands on a walkway talking
about how he landed
in the unfamiliar mountains of Colorado.

A winter story. (He was the proverbial fly
in the bowl of Denver airport.) He was,
he says, a stranger traveling townsfolk offered

inappropriate advice and direction to.
"You need a place to stay, don't you?
Go here," he says he was told.

And mimicking his anonymous advisors,
he holds out his empty hand
as if offering an address to his oldest daughter

who's on the hydrangea-lined walkway,
listening. Like anyone left behind,
she has long since learned to love an absence.

It's dusk, and in the evening of her ears
his absence takes on the shape of his voice
telling her his tale.

He isn't the hero, exactly.
Just a center
to which the anonymous are easily drawn.

The way the gaze of one looking
at a painting is led by perspective lines
and light to a _____ or _____.

Perhaps they were drawn to him
by the lines of gesture his eyes made in looking
away from their faces, from their luggage carts,

from the indian-silver and turquoise earrings
many of the women wore,
and now from his own daughter,

from the walkway to his mother's house,
from the untrimmed hydrangea bushes,
from his own life, perhaps.

Like the townsfolk from another tale
who couldn't help but touch the Golden Goose,
or touch the last one to touch the goose,

"they came to me," he says
Like the boy who gathers his goose,
without troubling himself about the people

stuck in mid-gesture, hanging onto it.

A Grammar of Waking

1.

First, light
commands a dreaming
eye-open.

Against
this, the loud-when-hook-
ing woman

draws her
Levelor blinds closed.
That, and look

ing eyes
done dreaming. "Look back
at them. See

if they
are looking back at you."
(Radio

blink. A-
rhythmical. Red. Light.)
"Time to rise."

Sun, you
shine; little houses
draw your blinds.

2.

First light
commandeers my dream —
"I," and on

Sip Ave.
pavement, a deaf-mute
draws his arm

over
his head — that bearded
moon of no

respite.
(Ashy skin offered
against light.)

"Turn, face
the concrete beneath
you." Here's

one more
sky, close and someday
covering.

Tread light-
ly in this parish
of crevice

and crawl.

3.

First light,
ants, commas, doors, ears,
I, "O!" dreams

punctuate
my grammatical
sky of sleep.

A voice
I'll dream says, "Words are
much louder

than one
voice." Not enough to

keep out sound

and light,
to keep from waking,
to keep sleep.

Hungry
and articulate
syllables

graze the
field of this page. Eat
this white grass

and stone
and imperfect pitch.
Gobble

that first
articulation —
"Let there be

this…" Re-
make the sun his face
reflects   (and

    thereby
    also his dark-moon face),
and the light

against
which she draws her blinds
    (and thereby

    also
    her blinds, her hands, her
    drawing shut:

    her slight
    shift of string, her slow

pull, her latch;

sky-turned
eyes, her iris, her catch
of breath, quick;

her shout,
her mouth born of an
impossible

mouth made
of these syllables) —
in quiet.

ALAN GILBERT

Relative Heat Index

1.

Everything is capable of being broken.

The mast of a miniature ship
snaps off beneath a fountain's cascade.
Children are silenced by a desert

where steel shimmers in the heat.

Who called? What's the address?

You hand me slivers.
You hand me over.

Storm clouds gather west of the west.
Slumming time.

2.

What are the conditions of knowledge?
How is knowledge conditioned?

Does the spoon get placed inside the knife?

I thought I would leave it all behind.

Disassembling the architecture
to the hum of machines and electronics,
next door to an impregnable bank
staffed by young women wearing
large engagement rings.

Rubbing the eyes until a dull sheen develops,
as individual trademarks form
a universal language
piped into
an elevator full of galley slaves
rhythmically mimicking a long pull on the oars

while wearing silver mittens.

I got biscuits.

3.

I don't need to be disciplined any more.

The butchers of your children
are becoming indistinguishable from
the butchers of our children.

A brisk wind bends
the landscape blue,
where a train never
arrives on time,
out beyond the station
of the present's passing.

diverse   divested

Past the arteries of commerce,
   the roadside scenic vistas,
   the geographical markers,
   the easy-off/easy-on fast food restaurants,
   the vast migrations and reverse migrations,
   the burning trash in the distance,
   the rest areas,
   the ubiquitous warm night crickets.

All of it dark with history.

4.

Car exhaust and soot gradually turn
the public Christmas ornaments gray
where they hang from stoplights and lampposts
like a small-town 4th of July parade.

Wrapping a wounded TV with gauze and medical tape.

this word as word   that word as word
       inserted opaque and transparent
    perambulating yet crowding the airwaves

It wasn't true.

Decaying food slowly accumulated in the refrigerator.
B-movie zombies ate our brains, anyway;
and then used a Zamboni to make their escape,

    just as this page is taking too long to download.

I'm a big plastic bucket full of frogs at the market.

    Waiting for response… Waiting for reply…

5.

Where would you be without love?

Happy to lean against desire.

Information is not innocent, either.

Please bring the car around;
then watch the clowns spill out.

(After a certain point, I stopped counting.)

(I've stopped.)

(Stopped.)

Who's going to stop it?

6.

All beginnings are endings:
　　　some blue like tissue pulled from the box,
　　　some red like flesh torn from the bone.

starred　　　elusive

A TV mumbles through the floorboards.

　　　　An athlete appears on a cereal box placed
　　　　in a television show made into a movie
　　　　with a soundtrack by a singer who wears
　　　　the athlete's jersey in a video.

　　　　I read about the athlete, ate the cereal,
　　　　watched the television show, missed
　　　　the movie, heard the song, didn't buy
　　　　the CD, but checked out the video.

Poetry is not entirely unhappy
with its debasement.

The window's wide-screen projection
folded itself into an endless swollen summer.
Green sparks squirt where chips of time scatter.

There are good reasons to be suspicious of beauty.

7.

Readers are not fish to hook.
A knot eventually shakes loose.

A crack ran horizontally across the whole windshield,
trapping the light in quick glimpses.

Sailors discover the uniqueness of each port
within a network of global markets.

History's ellipsis
provides ephemeral names for highways.
Now, every trucker I see
reminds me of you, mom.

sidetrack   backtrack   bushwhack

A lawn burns black
around a house built of bones
in the valley of cancer.

8.

How did it get to be called public opinion?

Asking:
Who tracks the prehistoric flight paths of pterodactyls over New Jersey?
Who knows what it's like to be a girl?

On certain days, you can see all the way back
to a billboard behind childhood.

Unaccompany me.

Memory
rewrites
history
as
history
rewrites
memory.

All art
so far
occurs during
wartime.

9.

An economy before the gold rush
sweats the consequences,
puts in a railroad line,
and awaits the inevitable gamblers,
                        the samplers,
                        and the romantics
            with their decibels and old coins.

        Fire in the city and
        dry lightning on the plains
flash neon in front of history's gloomy hotel

that staggers along with an emptied revolver
in its pale hand,

straining at the limits of sense.

It can't be rebuilt,
no matter how many Hollywood celebrities smile and offer to pitch in.

Instead,
        construct elaborate stage sets.

10.

Channel-surfing through the sitcoms
to get to another commercial.

A professional driver on a closed course
crashed into a camera mount.

There are many angles to choose from,
though all have obstructed views.

I bobbed along for days
and ended up where I started.

The porch light remained obscure
and a sinister car still idled out front.

All the draft dodgers now want to make war,
propping up a ladder that extends to nowhere —

> the small space of silence between the cricket's leg and wing
> where Apache helicopters bring the stuttering news.

11.

—for K. P.

A drink cart accidentally overturned
while the plane taxied,
triggering the inflatable yellow escape slides.
Dogs howled in the cargo hold
as their owners slid by.

It's impossible to tell where the river ends and the ocean begins.
Garbage barges break the water's smooth surface.

How much force can a building withstand?
What power does knowledge confirm or deny?

Seat cushions may be used as flotation devices
in the event of an emergency water landing.

A sudden storm eager to reach its destination
ignored the traffic signals synchronized on a grid.
In the morning, workers were already repairing the roof.

Sometimes love presses down hard.

You can take away the father.

Reprise the role.
Revise the rule.

12.

A virtual weather map plots
geography in a digital expanse
of history's frequent wardrobe changes
filmed through a green glass bottle
washed up on shore
where the dark imperium gathers its troops.

Cities shift their concrete features
to accommodate an influx of people and goods.
The local flora changes its hue.
An irradiated lake glows genially
at twilight,

as bathers splash around its soft, sandy edges.

The self makes stupid;
most silence is not profound.
Wrapping a hamburger with this text
will render it partially illegible.
A small pile of bricks waits to be made
into a cash register that also bakes pizzas.

Rain slickens the pavement outside.
Faulty wheels lose a little of their grip on the surface.

13.

Fiction binds throughout the day
and surrounds the manor house with torches

that also reflect in an office building's
revolving glass doors,
                        the dirty windows,

      just as a serial poem never starts over.

A streetlamp patchwork of glittering shadows
paves a take-out window's S-curve
                              hot asphalt
                        for the drive-thru soul.

The street quiets down
after a garbage track hauls off the page.

            Then another one
[repeat]
      takes its place.

14.

A meteorologist eats his way forward

to the sound of an electric can opener
and an out-of-tune piano,

the rain *ping ping ping* against a tin roof.

A concrete retaining wall
sags in the wet earth,
                splattering mud sunspots
            spun from a dentist's cruel vinyl chair.

What I knew before
doesn't seem worth knowing now.

        The next wave is Pepsi's latest advertising campaign.

Look for big branded pandas to float across a gray sky
or encircle a school of submerged dorsals.

15.

       Phantom limbs close the ivory lid
       on a nation's looped lullabies.

Temporal hamhocks thaw
amid a swirl of global sands
that jam the guns of empire
lost and regained.

A voice stuffed with glass
is a claim against lore —

       laying a tongue down on the tracks,
       laying down tracks on the tongue.

There's an uninvited guest
called hope who lounges
on the couch watching TV all day
and eats the remaining food
in a refrigerator

       that's periodically lapped by a rippling wake.

16.

Who's left picking up the check
written on a doctor's messy prescription pad
that transcribes the daily negotiations with power —

    (code name: Robin Banks)

— an atomic drift into oncoming traffic
from the McDonald's to the mall?

The newscaster's pancake makeup slowly melts
beneath harsh studio halogens.

Billboards clustered on a commuter highway
topple each other like dominos.

That nurse has handcuffs and a knife.

    The rest is rendered irrelevant   inconsequential,

which is different from just vanishing
into the world.

17.

History is a constant ringing in the ears
like locating a house in a tornado
with stars outlined in pink marker
unfixed in the sky above.

Fuel vapors make palm trees jiggle
in the distance.
Voices inaudibly argue
on the other side of bulletproof glass.

stamped   branded

I remember planned obsolescence:
    the shoddy paint job,
    the bad haircut,
    the kitchen sink full of dirty dishes.

Where do I belong
beneath all the cross-stitching?

            An x-ray peers through
        a defective heart
                    glowing on a barium screen.

18.

~~winter sun~~   ~~reptile museum~~

A winter sun in the reptile museum

    totes Budweiser in a rubber cooler

and gets plastered with metaphor
                or culture,

    with culture as metaphor and material.

What's natural?

Long gone past literal.

Poetry's images slip,
because I'm all wet.

19.

This is not a jam band; it's a dance band.

Illiteracy is a discourse.

The radiator heats the front half of the room.

The car bomb's engine was later found on a nearby balcony.

Any questions?

Famous is a relative category.

The blood flow stops once the wound begins to close.

Please check server.

Antelope twitch their ears at a salt lick.

Pull back the floorboards to discover what rots beneath.

What are the five things you can't live without?

A snarling dog rears back on its haunches.

I have some perspective on this.

It seems, EKG, as if you must have a strong heart, too.

Satellites photograph license plates from space.

Nice to meet you.

Defective O-rings were not the sole cause of the explosion.

20.

A cracked ruler takes time's malic measure
in a submarine built for one
with salad bar and dim searchlight included.

Marvelous aquatic creatures push their phosphorescent snouts
up against the compression-resistant glass
to relieve the tedium of unending seafloor dark and cold.

Insomnia's foundling skull lurches into the night,
as the fatal vessel methodically chugs along
in its quest for myth and dollars.

21.

The plastic needle drops below empty,
with no gas station around for miles,

 and its punch in the face,

 its boot on the neck of the producers.

There's no music in the desert,
except the contrails of jets.

 Literal
 crow's nest;
 literal
 widow.

The burgundy gleam
of an oil well's rusty lure

lies face down in the snow.

22.

Clowns are always
in a box.

Every child is first abandoned
before the law.

The clinking links
of a thick metal chain
run quickly through a pulley.

History loosens the bowels,
and a stack of books
gets knocked to the floor.

    Nothing is gathered up.
    Nothing finds its way home.

One-eyed styrofoam mackerels swirl
in a flooded empty railway yard,

    where blind conductors perform
    from a soggy script.

23.

Both the cows and the pasture are engineered for efficiency.

Fastening a camera to a gun turret.

Looking at a light
doesn't always reveal its source

    or its substitute for memory.

I found the hair dryer's design practical, efficient, even.

    Days tumble to the bottom corner
    of a tattered calendar. Words
    jostle and blur on the page.

This fire is not cleansing.

It overloads the circuits,
their fissures, and other
rooms to roam
            on a feedback tundra.

from *Construction Papers*

the pianist looks like an airline pilot who's afraid to land,
arguing for a love through logic; a series of black and white keys
establishing himself through this argument and not through love
maybe, become, to be
near the border with Shenzhen
an island of white cranes surveys the city tip

the nervous waiter in the Mandarin Hotel is young and polished.
flowers come out of small vases in the clipper lounge, established women
whisper sharply over tea perfumes the soft immediate
"we have the chance to be alive"

a Filipina maid is painting her face for church on Sunday. the birds are well
        stocked in
the trees outside. later she will meet with friends at City Hall where they
        will sit on the
pavement and talk. her employers have given her a Seiko watch for
        Christmas but she had
wanted to go home.
there is no going home
the Japanese girl in the English boarding school lights fire to the toilet
        paper
in the bathroom the fire alarm is going off

hot and sour nights the expensive wife playing tunes on underground rubies
she can't escape and let her heart down
, heavy wings, the heart she believes an infra red gun is aimed at her
from another penthouse
"release yourself"

forty Burmese women silently flip their wrists as they wrap cigars in a large,
        dark, cool barn
"your adventure is about to begin!"
in the air-conditioned Mall of America a couple disappears in the large
Rainforest Café, beneath oversized butterflies, bright hot spotlights and dis-
        posable dolphins

Hakka ladies in curtained hats collect garbage in the mornings
in the hills behind the house, large brown jars hold human ashes while
the wife of the house types absent all day. Working to connect the
homeless heart,
"so when I was five I knew enough to say so my father's dead. I didn't know
what that meant exactly, but I knew it was different from going on a busi-
ness trip"

the Berber man knows all about Rome and takes the tourist girl to the ruins
after beer,
buying her watermelon they spit seeds into history "and after meeting my
parents we will
go to the blue people in the desert and drink tea in their tents" he tries kiss-
ing her
in the haphazard haze of construction, bones of foundation left out in the
open
an island of multicoloured cranes surveys the city's tip near the border with
Shenzhen

part of the factory is left charred and black after the factory burned down in
Ngau Tau Kok
a woman walks past with her bouncing daughter in a pink party dress
no, nothing hurts, time must be brave

I will take my daughter to Ohio to show her there's more
to the world than this
even though she thinks she's independent
maze or web
another girl lost in re-memory echoes of Thai trains and American cereal
until she remembers there can be a way out

"this city is brand new. seven years ago this was not here. we have all left
        our homes to come here"
planet bound by strings of the money purse the train from Shenzhen is
        filled with men in similar white sleeved shirts
"if you work with us, I will bring you a monkey from my hometown. we
        will work together and play together."

"you have to cater to the market to be an artist and stay alive"
a thousand birds she doesn't see from the terrace of the Ladies' Recreation
        Club squawk in protest,
"fishing ships stranded in a desert that not long ago was part
of the Aral Sea. The Aral is drying up because of human intervention
in its ecological balance."

JOHANNES GÖRANSSON

The Last Instrument

The speed of horses. The steel of cars. The black of flash. The glass of hands. The steam of skin. The scar of lips. The dance of blights. The neighs of teeth. The road of sand. The road of run. The road of raw. The wheels of stars. The crash of hair. The kiss of stares. The breast of blue. The pluck of screws. The little little space between very and large. The little little race run from here to there. The bare snare growing out of the clothes. The hooves the skin the dance the dance of blights. That's how you learn how to play the instrument you wear around your neck. You have seven seconds.

Imitation

In a world alive in imitation
The letters on the page imitate language
The insects are landing on the page to imitate letters
The trees pretend they exist
The bicycles chatter
I am imitating myself
This is reflected perfectly
In the windows around me, the world
Alive in imitation, alive with
The art of quotations and I forget my next line
Everything returns to what it is.

Observation

Oh look,
a flock of kayakers
out the window

the "the"
"the"
the

there is a comma
to the wall
a wall
wall

"Oh look,
a flock of kayakers
out the window."

I Have Folded This Letter in Ten Places

Once for that time we met
  but did not speak
Once when I thought of you
  while opening a container of matchsticks
Once while ordering a drink
  for someone neither of us knows
Once just before sunset and we each disappeared
  at the moment of recognition
Once while boarding planes, me for Oslo
  and you for Spain
Once in line at the bank depositing checks
  you at the beginning
  and me at the end of the line
Once while selecting grapes at the local grocery
Once while I sat at a table writing
  and it was either you or somebody else
  I saw while writing the last line
Once for some other reason
Once in a dark theater where I imagined
  the lines spoken on stage
  were spoken by you.

Closed Discussion about the Future

(Diving over the vibrating floor.)

There is the sonic photon gone violet.

A shredded nuance engagement, and my original reactions:

(The waves are said to be "bluer" toward O.)

Wave crests and increased frequency

(The wave crests also spread outward with the passage of time.)

Average the proper motions. But I think my hand is moving closer —

Redshift and distance for extragalactic nebulae,

The triangles formed by our galaxy; those I deny for a

Sunken doormat, the booming chairman

I cannot separate from the primary stars, or the nearby pillow

With white flecks upon it. (The syncopated lock describes

The sore ankle.) I ask for a cheekbone.

Or adopt the peeling wallpaper of a capsule.

2.

The colloquium of two words;

The beauty product's flaming planet;

The mercurial ensign;

The brittle fortune cookie passing

(From mouth to mouth);

The telephone's sullen actuality.

Suppose we encounter a beach whose sand forms a smooth surface…

3.

(knock)

"The historian of multiple realities is here to see you now."

The sufficient equation of any given instant;

The thermodynamic;

The sodium line. Two kiwis and reliable organs;

(A substitute guar gum response

Delivers the syncopated fondue plate,

An illuminated, desirous forest of literal leaves.)

Combing the fireside chat, the bundled flowers

Were mailed yesterday (as was the alarm clock). An inadequate gearshift

Where the monsoon became real.

(We are a "group"; you have been "groped.") Bored with the lake

The water rises from the mechanism to the surface. The disengagement

Possesses a total allure of black dresses.

4.

And brings me to my original subject:

The sleek, silver, refrigerated, silicon embrace

Of winter. A little conversation inside,

An ugly ghost of ridden colors. The clouded monopoly chanteuse

Shows a curvaceous tail. (An audience's delight is

Suspended in the act of its own making.) A lucrative morphology to a sentry

And his secrets, the pains of a old yellow bulb:

I feel like I'm wearing "acid lipstick." (No, no.) A blasted fax.

(A sigh or gasp.) Viola fade out. My own software

The sonar contribution, the unglued sea's hum kills the string:

My city. My streets. My lights.

The moon's mellow swarm spoken to a focus group

Slit the red mood. His lips plunged to her nape.

Before the day's solipsistic crooner behaves badly

I wish I could offer a collective response, or regenerate the meaning,

Blow the dime. (Your ribs are one by one.) Fuming plumes

Desiring the air raid, indifference's tree-lined charade and mountain

Is a moneyed feeling.

(Can I resist tonight's freak-out syndrome,

Achieve a synthesis?)

(Dine on watches?) Think:

Extinct popsicle. (blow-drying)

Disbelief miming

The foreshadowed menthol event,

Crusaded through the cubic habitat

My sferic moment

I scratch on the surface:

(I am responsible.

I am responsible.

I am responsible.). Bubonic dispatch, ether's opposite

Trans-Atlantic carlift.

Understanding the thump. Not to mention the remember quotient.

(Am I seeing you

Or is this a recording device?) "Ten black squares" surveying

The "Swiss" abyss.

"Language will become concrete in our discussions."

Five Men

There were five men walking down the street, when suddenly
it started to rain in awkward musical forays
into the faces of shopkeepers.
Yesterday, I realized the reason we've been avoiding
each other might have to do with
our inability to keep down
the malt liquor produced in this town.
Finally it started to rain.
The droplets fell against the shopkeepers' daughters'
faces, their maidenheads running in the streets.
Later there was a hanging and everyone drank
open-nosed from the casks of gothic fiction.
Not only were there five men involved in the dispute,
there were five disputes, five deputies, and five girls.
Notaries arrived too late and the silver and linen
were sullied by gulls who were lured by the unclaimed hymens.

Also, there were five windows.
Nobody knew where they had come from.
Everyone felt outwardly gleeful but silently ashamed,
and this shame made us whole again.

JENNIFER KNOX

Chicken Bucket

Today I turn thirteen and quit the 4-H club for good.
I smoke way too much pot for that shit.
Besides, mama lost the rabbit and both legs
from the hip down in Vegas.
What am I supposed to do? Pretend to have a rabbit?
Bring an empty cage to the fair and say,
His name's REO Speedwagon and he weighs eight pounds?
My teacher, Mr. Ortiz, says, I'll miss you, Cassie,
then he gives me a dime of free crank and we have sex.
I do up the crank with mama and her boyfriend, Rick.
She throws me the keys to her wheelchair and says,
Baby, go get us a chicken bucket.
So I go and get us a chicken bucket.
On the way back to the trailer, I stop at Hardy's liquor store.
I don't want to look like a dork
carrying a chicken bucket into the store —
and even though mama always says
Never leave chicken where someone could steal it —
I wrap my jacket around it and hide it
under the wheelchair in the parking lot.
I've got a fake ID says my name's Sherry and I'm 22,
so I pick up a gallon of Montezuma Tequila,
a box of whip-its and four pornos.
Mama says, That Jerry Butler's got a real wide dick.
But the whole time I'm in line, I'm thinking,
Please God let the chicken bucket be OK.
Please God let the chicken bucket be OK.
Please God let the chicken bucket be OK.
The guy behind me's wearing a t-shirt
that says, Mustache Rides 10¢.
So I say, All I got's a nickel.
He says, You're cute,
so we go out to his van and have sex.
His dick's OK, but I've seen wider.
We drink most of the tequila and I ask him,
Want a whip-it?
He says, Fuck no — that shit rots your brain.
And when he says that, I feel kind of stupid

doing another one. But then I remember
what mama always told me:
Baby — be your own person.
Well fuck yes.
So I do another whip-it,
all by myself and it is great.
Suddenly it hits me —
Oh shit! the chicken bucket!
Sure enough, it's gone.
Mama's going to kill me.
Those motherfuckers even took my jacket.
I can't buy a new chicken bucket
because I spent all the money at Hardy's.
So I go back to the trailer, crouch outside
behind a bush, do all the whip-its,
puke on myself, roll in the dirt,
and throw open the screen door like a big empty wind.
Mama! Some Mexicans jumped me!
They got the chicken bucket
plus the rest of the money!

I look around the trailer.
Someone's taken all my old stuffed animals
and Barbies and torn them to pieces.
Fluff and arms and heads are all over the place.
I say someone did it,
but the only person around is Rick.
Mama is nowhere to be seen.
He cracks open another beer and says,
What chicken bucket?

Well, that was a long a time ago.
Rick and I got married
and we live in a trailer in Boron.
We don't live in a trailer park though —
in fact there's not another house around
for miles. But the baby
keeps me company. Rick says I'm becoming
quite a woman, and he's going to let mama know that
if we ever see her again.

God Gave Safe Passage to the Animals through His Forest of Bright Spectrums

You're searching for some [blue bird] thing in the living room, but you're not sure what [blue bird] it is — you woke up here, in your pajamas, holding your pee, feeling small and looking for some [blue bird] thing. Whatever it is, you can't leave without [blue bird] it as your briefcase feels eerily light, so you check the bedroom [blue bird], the kitchen [blue bird] — you tear the whole house [blue bird blue bird] apart until your family locks you out for acting nuts. From the porch, you watch how the sun coming up shrinks the small clouds of mist wandering around the yard like stray cows — dividing them once, then again, then piff. You hear an infomercial blaring from the neighbor's TV, but can't make out what they're [blue bird] selling. Is it time to scour the perimeter? Leave no stone unturned? Let's start at the corner tavern? "You won't find this [blue bird] thing anywhere," says the cat coming home from the night, "but in the shadows — which are too full, too fat, of [blue bird] it, and like me, they're sleepy," he yawns and three azure feathers pop out his pink mouth.

Pastoral with Internet Porn

These naked girls really love animals.
The lush green lawn seems greener when-
ever they're around. And to think father spent
his final days dribbling on about how heavy
cream flowed upstream when he was a lad,
how an orphan girl's hot biscuit was the best
fluff a coal jockey'd hope to stuff with butter
he churned through his own voluminous tears. "Dad, we paid a lot a money
for this house and that grass your chair's sitting on for
Christ's sake! These nice girls just want to wash
some donkeys at 100 bucks a pop for their cheer-
leading squad so try and relax and enjoy it!"

we'd yell in his ear — a blanched, waxy thing
ringed with hairs long enough to feel some
sudden shift on a wind a million years away
from this pretty, pretty place.

My Big German Bra

"Shut up and listen! Sit up
straight and stop simpering!
You call this supper?!
We wouldn't throw such food
to a dog in Berkenboorgsen!
I elbow you out of my way with a harumpf!
You call this a building?!?! Bah!
Your arms are full of schokolade!
My legs! They burst mit iodine!
Idjots! You know nothing
of crafting fine hood ornaments!
Silver women mit blondes hair
heaving their metal bosoms to the wind —
anchored down mit tight, wide straps!"

Cruising For Prostitutes

Motherfucker I just found out my boyfriend's a prostitute.
And we were saving up to go on a cruise.
I went and got all these brochures
from the travel agent on my lunch hour.
Billy introduced and that asshole never said,
"Steve, meet Chet — he's a prostitute."
I think I would've remembered that.
I met Chet's family once, and they all seemed
perfectly normal. Not like prostitutes
or people who'd encourage
their son to become a prostitute.

But now that I think back on it, he never seemed
like he was paying attention, and he never got
mad. I thought he was just
stupid. So now I don't know
shit: Are we still
going out?
Is he going to keep on
being a prostitute?
Did that motherfucker Billy
know? Does Chet's family
know? Who else
knows? Has he even looked at
any of the brochures I brought home? So
what's it going to be?
The Fun Ship or the Love Boat?

Son of The House of a Thousand Chandeliers

He was born gray as a trough of concrete,
under the sign
of SALE,

a million twinkly bees passing
over his big blank face,
all alone in the showroom

up to its roof in tumbleweeds
that sliced the sunlight inside to beige lace —
our baby hermit, on an asphalt island, adrift.

Time passed. A herd of limey deer
that handed out bullfight flyers in the parking lot
babysat, which shows you how low
the reservoir was.

They taught him the secret code
of hooves (tippy tap tap). He signed
the back of funny money
"Mommy" absent-
mindedly in thick pencil.

Some merchandise'd always fall
in the middle of the night
with a chongkrattleeringing!

and cast — without a shred of the night's
refractable light — shards of rainbows
all over his friends, the large tarp-covered humps,
and across the plate glass windows
black as the rare Floridian panthers

he would one day hunt and kill as coolly
as the cats themselves because he would be
very, very good at it.

Cho-Fu-Sa

It is what the river-merchant's wife writes her water-bound husband.
Cho-Fu-Sa being how far exactly? And will I ever know the truth

that is the distance one can travel away from the self to another
without breaking apart, until I have arrived, myself, white-hot

and thirsty, looking to tie one on in a three-syllable town:
the lover, the beloved, and the invisible animal they've raised

between them, into the wilderness between them of horns and roots,
blank sheets of paper mottled with light that sifts down through

leaf-cover, underbrush. How will I know this port town is the right
town until I stand at its wall, ripened by the miles I've walked

and sometimes sprinted with tears scattered down, like now, because
no matter how you reassure us, you will never come back to us

the same, but always wearing the other like a burning we must
reach through, the bright, new fever of home. Never mind that love

contracts the world, that if you bind your breath together, we are only
one breath away. Let us in. We have fistfuls of seed, foreign coins,

and gold string, blossoms and wishes, buttons that fell from your cuff.
Those days you were tenaciously single and uncertain, or

ecstatic with resolve, to hold out for the one, the town of two-in-one.
Where the swell rushes the shore nonchalantly, striking like a vow

until there's no more sand to strike upon. Let us in to lob our small
gifts above your path. The arms to fly out with generous abandon.

The hand to open. The hand to open. The hands opening as you pass.
If you should look back to find us scrambling behind you, sweeping

the floor for grain or confetti caught and freed by your veil,
who can blame us? No — embrace us, lock us into your town.

We won't be here much longer. Because this is the part when
you want to be alone, when you feed us to the tigers and kiss.

With Cheerful Speed

We were spinning ourselves into a rare dessert,
a delicate sugar helmet, deliriously scribbled, snow
that would melt on contact with that other intractable world.

French King Henry took to wearing a basket of little dogs
on a ribbon around his neck. One famous architect
sat in the vespertine light in the lonely brilliance
of one recurring idea: that acid-stained titanium wing,
that corner he meant for more than his dream —
what is there now? A vase, dust, a precocious child?

There are many ways of swallowing death for the stone
that it is. My mother liked me to hang from the upstairs
banister and sing opera through the railings. Cranking
all the windows closed, con brio, then reaching
the end of the hall, wanting an endless hall with more
windows to shut before the storm — this was
my mother's version of transport.

Some of us are looking for a smoother transition,
not a whiff of pain, no memories needed, no familiar tune
the name of a loved one, a movie star.

The English called it *sprezzatura*, the ability to think
an impossible lightness into the body and leap over
a mess of tombs thereby escaping your godbound
enemies or by the flourishes of a sword
cut the gown into a hundred bits leaving the woman
that had been so tightly bandaged in tulle more or less
naked not even nicked by the sword.
What woman suddenly stripped to a breeze
she had only felt on her hands and face
would not make that premarital leap? She is
the lucky beneficiary of another's studied
effortlessness. You will carry her across death
because you have matched yourself
to nothingness and she has not.

AMY LINGAFELTER

The Candy Poem

When you smoke with both hands all night, both sets of fingers smell,
which is why I love candy. Nasty

candy. Everything's coming up tart
and crunchy. I believe candy. I believe in America.
For example, I am an American, and I use a brass
paperweight when I'm working in my office with the windows open.
As a child, I ate candy before I ever smoked
in my office with the windows open. I've met a thousand
people, but I ate candy first.

I wish I had an office. When I was quite small, I wished
for an office, or to be homeless, or to be the child
of a broken home. I'm not sure how small.
Or to be a girl addicted to diet pills.
I believe we all had candy before we were
even made out of sperm,
before we were even souls floating
around in St. Raymond's Cathedral waiting to be
made out of sperm.

There is eating, and then there is eating (isn't there?),
And lately, I've been telling
myself there is no use eating in America.
I believe in Elvis Presley and candy, and sometimes,
I find myself crying. I wish I had long hair,

or more succinctly, I wish my hair
was growing out faster, so that I might cut it short again.
If you listen closely to girls, you'll see they always
know exactly what they're doing. Like with my hair,
like with the candy theory.

It's the dialogue of another world, not girls or candy,
but the distinct feeling I get that you don't believe
this is not a poem about candy. I guess
I'm just the dialogue of another world. And where are
other worlds? Outside the Milky Way. Uh-huh. This whole
world is full of hate and love,

And when we say "love," we mean… well, other people
can say it better than I can.
Though I can't think of any who will stand with candy,

and isn't it funny that in all these things, I have
not mentioned candy? Yes. And sleeping? Yes.
And the flavors of
"purple" and "red"? Sigh.

I've got lots of pictures of myself. I see cute men
everywhere. I want to tell them they're cute,
but they probably already know, which brings us

back to cigarettes and candy and what I firmly
believe in — we are all safe with candy.
We are all locked in a safe with candy.
I cried when I found that out.

The Grandmothers

If you can't accept the fact that
you're human,
then maybe you aren't human.
Take the grandmothers
whose eyelids no longer work,
no longer blink voluntarily,
and who have begun asking for whiskey.
Just because you can ask "How"
doesn't mean you have to ask "How."
And don't think "When"
is what you should be asking either.
Don't think if you ignore this and ask anyway,
and if you happen to get an answer
it will be satisfactory or correct
or satisfactory.
Take the grandmothers,
who have only just begun asking for whiskey,
but who began having babies at 14
in a time when and a place where
they were
neither teenagers,
nor pregnant.
So if you can't accept the fact that
you're human,
then the answers don't matter.
Maybe I am too young to be explaining
the grandmothers, explaining it to the grandmothers,
who cannot swallow, or blink to scoff at the idea.
This fact of listening
means nothing.

My Boyfriend, the Infidel…

My boyfriend, the Infidel, is dying of old age
So I am praying to Virginia Woolf to soften his heart.
I had to kill a lot of impulses to get to him & his point of misery.
A black cloud chased me with erotic intention then.
My vanity drove me to the ends of the earth
In search of nubile flesh & my runny little heart
Slid back & forth along the glamour axis
That is the Rivers' Divide — an iffy affair flecked with grief.
I fled to a Mexican isle just to lose my honkey pallor
Turn the faint & dirty mimeograph
Red of nipples, die on the line if I recall
There was a bandaged harem somewhere in the background
Brownouts, sparklers, girls with organic breasts
Ducking through oyster fog…
The subject of the mural was the Apocalypse & I think
You handled the destruction of the world
As gently as possible Larry I
Am really bawling now, can't get through —
We're both sticking to our guns
But I'm loaded really bombed, shot up
All night with the horrors though my cousin,
My gastroenterologist says I'm fine inside.

Blue Collar Holiday

And if I feel like a woman looming over Lautrec
with water weight & panties and murderous fuchsia underfoot
those dying balloons on Job's Lane sag around like saline breast implants
and pineal sunbeams sneak through my hair
dirty but focused as screwy detectives or plexiglass
I go to pieces in my adolescent pine
amid blackheads, seltzer, a cold front
falling into a decline
like ladies on the prairies used to
in the kleig-lit house with the deodorant cakes in the upstairs johns
and the foam core ass on *Bad Secretary* in the living room
and the foam core bird paintings in the kleig-lit kitchen
warm & endangered as an Orca whale float,
pollen & Coronas, in the foggy autumn
and the thin nude branches all snow-furred
like an x-ray of infant bronchitis. Wrist-slitting stuff.
My honey chapstick stinks of piss & menstrual sharkfear
but like the alpha male in Brownie troops ankled in mud
I sit tight, coping, & spit. The Mormons taught me
to have fortitude when I am in the right & right now
I stand stalwart as lung-colored support hose
in a French sex & deather for readers under twelve
My Indian name is "Little Hard-Core" I yank on a blue collar
since we have so many blue collar holidays
salute myself for alpinism — just being high really
& degrees of cousinage even misty like this

The Para-Olympic Legacy

Sometimes I look at people & think Jesus what happened here.
Race turns to me & speaks its rage & I
am dark with it. Like the troubled teen life
Of Farrah Fawcett or an orphanage saved
By a bikini car wash or Tony
pissing in the elevator, my *Affair to Remember.*
The original *Thomas Crown Affair* was much better
Than the mascara-streaked Russo pummeling Pierce
Brosnan's impervious chest.
The Heart's Filthy Lesson we call it.
An Infinity begins and backfires —
A stately bang against the universe
Crude and seminal like the Special Olympics
Or the heroine's false sense of invincibility — I just
Want to grab her by her anorexic shoulders & moan
I know, I know, but Snow White she seems so easy
One kiss & she really "came to life." Slut.
I guess I was expecting rain, suspecting
Tony when he was being so good.

Wu Gambinos

I feel strongly about sanctity & wash
With Flex & the oily Ives of March,
Nap hoarsely in florid throat tones,
Am consumed with Bright's disease —
A love flared yesterday in flushing queens
Expired amid diet ginger ale & racy glads.
The sweaty nimbus blasting down on
The new whatever in the ghetto.
You go to those places & you get sick.
I was peopling bald love in nightmares
To rail against the sterile, the Young
Women's Christian Association.
My mama told me: your best friend is mascara
& you don't have to walk a "mascara,"
Get let down like whores misled by angels
In self-defense magazines-that sort of thing.
I mean last week if you'd watched the Godfather
Come down, a blue-maned prince in speedos
& somebody forgot the acting lesson,
Cried "uncle!"… Famiglia values —
It's always about recovery isn't it?
I couldn't wrestle a broad
Gestural field into being, failed a pee test
& then they paged me that Irving had been thrown
From his Triumph.

Stick-up

Thanks for the novel on Catherine the Great.
I was greatly relieved to discover there are fates
Far worse than blackness, the clap. Though
Nobody knows what they are...
& so come to shepherd me across a stretch of wicked terrain
More limp-wristed wives black-balled from the Bath & Tennis Club.
"O the girls used to dot their *I*s with hearts" & their hearts just
Break like chocolate, sharp & warm
& exclusive like after-swim bowel movements.
White Castle burgers. High-class poo-poo.
I am assaulted by a cohesive mass
Of confidence & steal lines, long & thin
Like stringy hemorrhoids or cowboy ties.
I choose not to think of it as plagiarism but as "synchronicity" as in:
Christ was born on a bank
Holiday & died on a bank
Holiday & I'm worrying about my hedge fund
When a voice blurts out, You could have got salvation,
Tricolor pasta if you had waited but since you acted
The way you did you get nothing!

Like Beatrix Potter,

Wittgenstein held a sweaty mother once too
    with an armature of lines
Oh god yes & didn't he feel that like a kid

playfully moved by a tornado
& plopped down into a watered-down cotillion,
    truant semester of brain nerves & deviled eggs

    & so we are awful little people with awful little dreams...

Well, don't get in a fuck about it
thinks Beatrix crapped out on a diagonal,
with car swerves & madcap shooting
    at the height of a person's heart

Anyway the glamour & crash of Wittgenstein without blood
or Black Russians

Delineates the helixes of Beatrix
    "my speedy dessert season"
    An armistice wrested from the dying bunnies
& splayed like the fourth of July

Her old bean primed for love & petrified
like spring girls in weight rooms at 14
Hold on pussy hold on
    There you go. Now you're fine.

Beatrix's affections return tenacious
& slow like spanked kids or continental drift
All this & she is deaf

Warner Bros. Newest Thriller *Valentine*

Anything I do will be an abuse of somebody's aesthetics.
I index moccasins on the web.
I used to translate Xenophon during the typhoons
But now I live in "far-off" Chelsea where my god forsakes me
Several times a day. They say social anxiety can hurt careers
Though mostly I am suffering from intestinal complaint, ghetto-bred
Inertia. "From the dark bastions of the UN, a sick flush."
I read it in the papers, the *New York Times*.
I fortify myself, douse my sushi with "liquid aminos" spray,
Fly Lufthansa. And you're flying past in an Adirondack chair
With soiled pubes & argon lighting — a fluid mai tai
Coursing through this land of nausea & bric-a-brac.
Anglican & very high I am, the consort of a genuine Black Forest
Paterfamilias — the Bavarian Lift face & throat crème
Splashed down in spermy smears, peals
Of screaming laughter as an orchestra dressed in skivvies
Accompanied a chorus of Yodelling Alpine maidens…
Skit night at Christine's & everything seemed a waitress
In the throes of athletic lovemaking or centennial
Valkyrie slumbers with you, indecently pink
& tan like swatches of rarified turkey burger
& me shrinking beside you & you Nivea-slick skin
"Really & truly I don't care what you do with me."
So I put on my little Lederhosen & started to walk.

"Larry Kept Saying Primo Levi Was an Accident"

Larry kept saying Primo Levi was an accident
& "about as scary as a glass of orange juice"
Orange Jews he kept saying when I asked for a raise, high
& seedy love to be gathered & dispersed
like diaphanous monks or politics
I never wanted to fight the war against MS
I am trying to live with myself in critical care
in Chelsea room #224 minus the bladder control of Cub Scouts
Did a dog fall out that window I sorta understand
child leashes on Manhattan streets
like bravura brushstroke, one little dash right here
& it's all over I defend blindly whatever
brings me money. Well there's nothing
wonderful in that I really should stop
with the queer diction it's 1999 but I got laid
in heaven & must rage on as such
against the dying of the light, etc.

The Shark Wrangler Goes to Church

Because Americans love seafood I can
Be invited inside the national chain of my choice
But today all the chains are failing & the weather's crushing
On all the hotties in the Flowers District I wish
We were all dead & tight & cleanly rise like scabs
Or a smart Lord & Taylor window even less attractive
The more you scrub, the closer you get to the superhero inside
A/k/a The Spiderwoman in our queer version
Of *The Chocolate Wars.* What I wouldn't do for Sam
Cooke. Laying eggs for me & nobody else.
But here the man's trouble. He's been to my house.
Milk protein straight from the subway midday on a Sunday.
The Turks are not with me now & this thing keeps breaking open.

Don't Let Me Eat Dinner

Smoking & juvenile obesity are not uncommon in unhappy people
Especially in *Alice Doesn't Live Here Anymore*
(her kids do but that's a different story)
The sky low-slung & beer-colored with curling tufts of dry ice smoke
Amid Alaskan, if not "Alaskan," snow & billboard shots
Of Kate Moss in those jean ads when she was, like, age two
I'm not eating again until I am that thin
I subsist on squab filets, "turn toward purple colas" (diet) & upset them
As in a poem that springs a chubby when the lights go on
Ask me what these days & nights are like, Tits!
Like a blast of cold fir green air around human irises.
My nerves, my nerves! Mama take this pepper spray from me —
I can't defame the minions to-night
On this isle we have with the statue of liberation
I am not a mature audience, possess the sexual mores
Of estrous chinchillas in the remote & humorless
Hinterlands of Jersey City but neuters are never happy either
Oh my life is a string of meaningless affairs I can never go back
Whatever becomes of me, I shall never use this lavatory again.
I am so drunk.

No Matter What Sign You Are

The Asian Century wasn't supposed to start like this.
I put down rebellion with good ketchup violence,
Some exiled text from *The Manchurian Candidate*
In what became a ruptured aneurysm, a grande dame honored at lunch.
Nasdaq fell & I'm at home with the kids, my beautiful Ramone Dee Dee
& my shy mother Sandy. A mother's love is so special.
Hey Mama my heart belongs to you... & The Sherry Netherlands also
But the bellboy at The Sherry Netherlands is tough love
& smarts with a Chinese visibility like hats. A dream & I was sketching
In this heinous poem, I cried Larry, that I was failing
Gorgeously. He stuck a thumb in my ass, said "sleep it off kid."

Vanishing Point

Depressed like cabin air & passing out
peach-tinted hygiene manuals
    on West Side Highway I lead men on
like the Virgil of the garment district:

Now this lovely structure on your right
is baby's jeans & a struggling pyramid of girls & oh
well I understand his orphans with my gun like cinema verite

shot through with lower-functioning inmates —
    with the "inkings of Scandinavian malaise" & whatnot
I go see art & feel priceless but to be a good sport you have to lose
    & lose value like junk bonds he likes to "sit back & watch 'em grow..."

The Met stuffed with alabaster tits I left alone, sexy & mightily un-Dutch

Mastered, set fire to a batik picture
    of Mother Chelsea the Pitiless who wasn't sickle-
    Cell white & incontinent & Dia-funded

I stood in his cloud shirt by myself

cursed to stalk the night through all eternity & original so on
Through the small ballet company of stocking runs & upset

Nuns down Sixth Avenue, John Wieners,
the Americas breaking apart so I can feel this sinuous & partial wind
    like Lyme disease with a drip in the arm & the sky is falling.

Tom Brokaw

Tom Brokaw is a beautiful person.
   By beautiful I mean communicating disease

as in the Pythagorean theorem swiped at by mud-covered tribes
The incident of my subtraction Tom thought. White
as Rauschenberg's supposed rudeness

Forget that night & your wet socks. Low-flying engines. She'll never hap-
pen again.

               Did he jump, Tom, did he! And it's fall in the Southern hemi-
sphere
               Of towels, gross raging, the shits again

                  Febrile men-wept, whacked out: I've got to go big dis-
tances…

   Well-hung & snow-white trash.
   The furniture was heavy failing also.
   Is this physics or ambivalence?   No matter.   Tom remains
sequestered,

                                        loves them amidst news
                          of child abuse & lake effect snow. His news, a
   series
of vibrations their sadness
   & visions bring into relief.
Beyond toejams, landfills, caviar.   The despondent correspondent
   pushing all those riotous grey sheep
            into a quiet form of media.

"Colors" starring Patti, Grandma, & me at twenty-five

Wherever you go there you are like Patti Smith's shoulders
placed in this cold century with a virility that lacks self-esteem
Paco says hang on & flourish

like Grandma Moses   I use her little legs & go to town
making scenes in which a dirty lover breaks
    down   blushing assailants
in bra-training films.   My college heartsprain
    harried & in sympathy with the damning empire

Guess I'll grow up to be as pink & mean as God
with spareribs, a Dutch vocabulary lesson
    which makes my uncle see red
eyes closed to people's moorings, spoiling it

& a kid's liver gets smacked in on a jungle gym
vibrates beneath a bright sexual state
of the union address
    Poor Paco. Poor Jim Dine.

Audit trails are here again & I have never
smashed a black widow
    myself Forcefed horsemeat
    out in the sticks or
stark mad on the sidelines, some

brownies skip forward as in a fugue singing Horses through
with Orangina, head gear, the "Hispanic child rack"
transmuted into nerves & glory & this

the ruinous work of nostalgia
in my august opinion
    in a turgid march
or my dream of becoming alive on a turnpike
like a two-ton hussy the way I
don't fall in at weigh stations
    lighting the endless white race

with elbows, lymph systems my valentine
& Grandma Moses sweating in an infinitely soft asylum

Stations of the Crux

Mainly I liked walking through the water
which reflected the sun like a mirror
and burned us quite often.
                              One short guy
taught me what it's like to be a sailor.
We later found that the butter-cancer
had spread all over, and though I went
supplicatingly to the grave
of Mr. Dragoo, fronds playing on my back,

I still likely had no soul.
They didn't know what to say about that,
except that with the decanter all things
may be possible. Look at its swirling silver
design, the design it imparts to your tea
in the light.

Massive Stoner

Though it all floods back to you
and an ascendance to grace is almost like an ascendance to sleep
and the chameleons will still stick purring to your walls,
this suit may have to be settled and worn elsewhere for a while,
the mental exercise sedimenting, the apple crisping in your hand,
the guitar repetitive and understated,
and we will lower our expectations and lower them until
we see you with nothing on a flat beach but some alcohol
in a coconut and the Life of Ecclesiastes
and your red swim trunks, ready to happen to make it happen.

But what you massacred into the tablature was this: Dear cops,
don't ever touch me, I will rise in the air like a phalanx of scorpions.

To the Horizon

—A beautiful bird we rinsed the soap from gently.

—A bathroom so elaborately rigged you learned a lesson
  about heaven and hell.

But how I'd fucked up there anyway, and was returning home
empty-handed.
                —A problem I solved by not eating.
But three blocks later the same shell-car, more anemic and oxidized,
burning by the road.

And if we can work something out or get a bus to drive there
we can party all winter, blow everything in the river.

Excluding one light, corner room: looking at the picture one can tell who's
      home,
and so forget about looking in; and put off moving
for a couple more seasons.

The Bird

Sun trailing alongside —

Trying to find something to meet with —
Bird holds in the air before the car's moving radiator —

Who knows what your life is like, really?
Destruction subsumed in the idea of swimming;
a soft-voiced apology for the old black temple.

The bird was freed, or fired.
He is tragic to you now flash by flash
and is blotted up with praise.
"He'll warble throughout his cynosure–forever.
Straining at the leash, golden retrouver.
Half the night darker, then half lighter.
Singing, staying and not dying again."

Paying for this,
each moment a new bird,
you touch your partner's shoulder —

"The chirp, and then alight.
All day, in flight.
No love deserves a home."

It's all good, but that speaker can never return.

Sweetness

One time the moon was full and — our blind selves! —
we were confronted with a round fertile dance
and I remember that proposition
but not how we moved in response.
Out on the course the clay enjoyed posing,
being looked at, composing.
The guide held pictures of instants and snakes,
the boy touching the hamburger sadly,

the fake pond blowing by the interstate.
There were days, reclining in the car with her,
she would just reel out in tears
accenting the consummation.
How can it be unsteady and still hold me
like it cares for me? Meaning my body. I
wandered into the loud wind. In retrospect,

gripping the armrest in the feature film, I knew
she wanted to live in some external paradise.
Positive eons and negative eons
shaping the dancing homunculus. Sweetness
and darkness outpacing every lion. In that me

who am in the end the what I had shown
in order to get there.
Some part of this casket got left in the factory.
"I'll go get it, I'll be right back," I told them,
creaking past the tissue box
down through the winding essay
and yet to bring each memory to the table
or carry it to the dais —
"he recognizes distantly his intransigence,"
the rattling of the chest as a cue for more stillness,
the mother holding the hem, father
filling the sidelines. Starting
my piece of crap brown car in the piece of dusk,

the language of the actual question
such a tragedy in verse
and in our time to make the transition
there's no way to bring with us all creation
in the honest form one would hope for —
the half-life of each bouquet going, the car
still charged tenaciously to the block,
our future children flickering
before the speakers, and when I speak I do
to drown or call you.

That Is the Way

I had thought I could say these words
but you had run across the street
and I could not go where you had gone

This is where it often ends
A moves towards B
only to find that B
was only pretending to be in a place
where A might reach it
No,
B has realized the shortcomings of the first place,
and though A may not realize them,
B has no intention of sharing
the secrets of the second place

This will affect the last count
if the light is bright enough
If not, it will make us anxious
(and I am sorry, there is no remedy,
maybe taking a drink of water, looking up
into the dark live oaks, but guarantees are not mine to give)

Because we are always A,
always in the middle of being left,
or if we should happen to be B,
it is only for a moment,
and a curtain falls over everything soon after,
gives no pleasure in the taking of that moment,
is almost surprised that pleasure was expected

As If I Knew

It was a good year, he says at the top of the new hotel, in the room always lit, in the room in which a television always plays *The Dahlia*, in which a flower is the voice of a death, what voice it can muster in the crackly noplace;

it was a good year, he says, lying on his bed, hands outstretched, in one hand the model of a small city — where we may find an apothecary ever to grind in a pestle, an architect to build Valhalla, an optometrist to let us Through — and in the other the wrapper from a box of cigars given to a box of friends;

it was a good year, if you take out the bad, he says, as the snow picks up, as predicted from blue fields on the edges of weather; and the guest can see less, but he looks less as one meeting begets another meeting, as more water is drunk, as a series of figures keeps him from his train;

in which the living room is empty till the murderer enters, the sound is running behind, mouths move, the ending will not satisfy;

if you take out the bad, you are left with the following figures, he says;

where we pray beneath the bells, where we play some old records when the houses are empty;

if you take out the bad, having loosened his tie, having dropped his shoes, having picked up the phone;

it was a good year, he says from the top of the new hotel, to his absent, to the Wood of Suicides, to the Bellhop;

in which a flower is a piece of candy, in which a face is a piece of contrast; the film may stop as an object may stop, mid-sentence;

if you take out the bad parts, sure it was fine, maybe with changes; the glass he has held will fall on the ground;

in which brambles grow at the scene of the crime, in which everyone knows, all the time;

goodness gracious, the killer done struck again

Here and There

This cash crop nation boasts one bridge
The bridge casts no shadow
Only a dotted line
I do not know the name of my companion
All that matters is the motion and the sound
I carry my heart behind a button
On that button float two toy ships
facing each other
two pieces of the same conflagration
Hush is the only word on our lips
in a country of souls and stolen stones
Here is my shining tin cup
Let something fall into it
that cannot be returned
Say a minute of your time
Say a file of misplaced certificates
that pop in the air before I can read them
that spin like coins
to the center of the earth
What's-His-Name asks a question
Two fishnet legs appear
to cross the ceiling of the struggle
to go away
I am going blind I say to myself
I am going blind
and no one will take me home

The Ascent

—for L. L.

When suddenly
out the window
there were two of them, then three
I did not name them
I did not know enough to try
There were signs that someone had been
Someone had placed a marker
a consecration
sometimes painted red or white
sometimes designated by a man from China
I picked them out
though the train was moving fast
picked them out and held onto them

You were not distracted as was I
You offered me a book
speaking of the maintenance of the mind
but the mind is just a copy of a thing made in heaven
It has been said to go off with a series of beeps
in hallways and kitchens
The order has swung like a pendulum
You were asleep as you said those things
You saw the cranes swimming
for the first time in their simple lives
You saw the ocean rising
with everyone inside it
You were comfortable letting go
just a snatch for fifteen minutes

I thought it might be nice to draw
take the drawing to the wall
make on that wall a picture
call that picture a well for the eyes
And then after that the museums
the traveling exhibitions

With luck I might become the sunrise
a wind of radiation
a blossom made from weariness
Will you follow me there
Will you tie yourself to my hand
ascend the slope

Biographies and Acknowledgments

Jordan Davis is the author of *Million Poems Journal* (Faux) and an editor of *The Hat*. He lives and works in New York.

Sarah Manguso is the author of *The Captain Lands in Paradise* (Alice James Books), which was named one of "Our 25 Favorite Books of 2002" by *The Village Voice*. Educated at Harvard and the Iowa Writers' Workshop, she is currently a Hodder Fellow at Princeton University.

*

B. J. Atwood-Fukuda lives and writes in Spuyten Duyvil, New York, and Woods Hole, Massachusetts. Her work has appeared in *American Letters & Commentary*, *Bamboo Telegraph*, and other journals. Her book, *Doggerel Camera*, a collaboration with photographer Jane Evelyn Atwood, was recently completed and awaits publication.

"The Wreck of the *Platonic*" first appeared in *American Letters & Commentary* and later appeared in *Great American Prose Poems: From Poe to the Present* (Scribner, 2003).

Jim Behrle edits *can we have our ball back?* and *70 Foot Rotating Dildo*. His work has appeared in *Fence, Slope* and *Cy Press Magazine*. His latest chapbook is *(Purple) Notebook of the Lake* (Braincase Press).

"White Album" first appeared in *Petticoat Relaxer*; "Beacon Arms" and "Goodnight, All You Ships at Sea, You" first appeared in *Let Me Turn You On* (Faux); "The Charm of the Highway Strip" first appeared in *Rife*.

Carson Cistulli is 23 and attended Columbia University and the University of Montana. He recently finished a manuscript entitled *Englished by Diverse Hands*, which was a finalist for the 2003 Fence Modern Poets Series judged by Peter Gizzi. He lives in Missoula, Montana, though is very soon returning to New England.

"34.57" and "42.24" first appeared in *The Hat*.

Chris O. Cook was dragged up on Long Island, New York, starting in 1978. He has degrees from Kenyon College and the Iowa Writers' Workshop. He's been a grocery bagger, costume store stockboy, video store clerk, locker combination changer, and standardized test grader. Chris has taught various English classes at U. of Iowa, Kirkwood, & (currently) DePaul. He lives in Chicago.

Del Ray Cross lives in San Francisco. He's also lived in Boston, Toledo (Ohio), Ann Arbor, Little Rock, and Charleston (Arkansas). He's in two sets of Poetry Espresso's Postcard Poems, with Cassie Lewis and Stephanie Young (and forthcoming with Tim Yu and Jim Behrle).

Del Ray's poems here first appeared in *Cinema Yosemite* (Pressed Wafer).

Katie Degentesh lives and writes in New York. Her poems and reviews have appeared in numerous magazines, including *Combo, Arras, Fourteen Hills, Fence*, and the *Poetry Project Newsletter*. She has an M.A. in English from the University of California at Davis, and keeps a blog of local observations at katied.blogspot.com.

Tonya Foster grew up in New Orleans and received her M.F.A. from the University of Houston. She lives in New York.

Alan Gilbert's writings on poetry, art, culture, and politics have appeared in a variety of publications, as have his poems. He lives in Brooklyn, New York.

Greta Goetz wrote *Construction Papers* as a means to constructively exit the fast-paced life of Hong Kong, where she grew up. Either we write our own histories, or they write us. On her search for the meaning of life (because neither working as a journalist at the *South China Morning Post* nor at the news desk of *Time* magazine gave her any answers worth keeping) Greta asked, "What is the point of all these words?" and suddenly found herself in Belgrade, Serbia, two years after the bombardment (testimony to further notions of reconstruction), where she converted to the Orthodox Christian church having "tasted" the Word (it is not enough to hear about, one must come and see and taste).

She won the Academy of American Poets Award at Columbia University where she graduated *cum laude* in Anthropology with a minor in Writing, and also won the George E. Woodbury Poetry Prize twice. Today she teaches writing and conversation at the University of Belgrade.

She hopes to testify to three words: hope, faith and love. May you all begin with Peace and end with Love.

Excerpts from *Construction Papers* first appeared in *The Hat*.

Johannes Göransson was born in Sweden but has lived in the US for the past 17 years. He has an M.F.A. from University of Iowa. His poems and translations of Swedish poet Aase Berg have appeared in *Jubilat*, *Conduit*, *Verse*, and other journals.

"The Last Instrument" first appeared in *American Letters & Commentary*.

Tim Griffin is editor of *Artforum International*.

"Imitation" and "Observation" first appeared in *Explosive*; "I Have Folded This Letter in Ten Places" first appeared in *Lingo*; "Closed Discussion About the Future" first appeared in *Fence*.

Cole Heinowitz is a poet and critic. Her poems have appeared in *6x6*, *How2*, *Mirage 4 Period(ical)*, *Factorial!*, *Readme*, *can we have our ball back*, and other journals. Her chapbook *Stunning in Muscle Hospital* was published by Detour Press in 2002. Heinowitz's critical work has appeared or is forthcoming in *Revista Hispánica Moderna*, and in the collections *Connecting Continents: Britain and Latin America, 1780-1900* and *"Sullen Fires across the Atlantic": Essays in British and American Romanticism*. She is currently an Assistant Professor at Dartmouth College, where she teaches Romantic literature, 20th-century American poetry, and the Gothic.

"Five Men" first appeared in *Stunning in Muscle Hospital*.

Jennifer Knox is the author of *A Gringo Like Me*, forthcoming from Soft Skull Press. She lives in Brooklyn.

Tanya Larkin lives in Somerville, Massachusetts, and teaches at the New England Art Institute in Brookline.

Amy Lingafelter is originally from Joliet, Illinois, and is currently a graduate student in Library Science at the University of Illinois in Champaign. She received an M.F.A. in poetry from the University of Iowa Writers' Workshop in 2000.

"The Candy Poem" first appeared in *Black Warrior Review;* "The Grandmothers" first appeared in *Crab Orchard Review.*

Jeni Olin received her B.A. and M.F.A. from Naropa University. She has published in such online and print magazines as *Jacket*, *Exquisite Corpse*, *can we have our ball back*, *The East Villager*, puppyflowers.com, *Hanging Loose*, *The Hat*, Angry Dog Press, *The Attached Document*, *Blue Books*, and fauxpress.com. She is currently studying to be a nurse at NYU.

Michael Savitz's poems have been published in *Verse*, *Denver Quarterly*, *American Letters and Commentary*, and other journals.

"Massive Stoner" first appeared in *Conduit*.

Max Winter is the winner of the Fifth Annual *Boston Review* Poetry Contest. He lives in New York City.

"As If I Knew" first appeared in *Jacket*.